Tummy Tickling Jokes for Kids

The Funniest Knock-Knock, Riddles, and Long Jokes for Kids

By J M L Designs

Table of Contents

Introduction

Hey kids! Sometimes we all need a good laugh now and then. In this book, I found the very best jokes for you to enjoy! There are some funny tummy tickling jokes that are sure to keep you laughing for days, the best knock-knock jokes in the world, riddles that will make you think long and hard, insanely clever long jokes, and some tongue twisters that'll keep you entertained. You could share these with friends and family; they're guaranteed to knock their socks off!

Is there an awkward moment at the dinner table? Crack a joke. Your friend seems bored and you want to make them laugh? Throw a fun tongue twister their way! Your sister feels sad and you want to cheer her up? Use a fun tummy tickling joke! There'll be endless hours of laughter and fun using jokes in this great book! Have fun!

Chapter 1: Tummy Tickling Jokes

The first chapter has the best tummy tickling jokes in the whole world! Read them out loud to friends and watch them break out into laughter.

WHAT WOULD YOU SAY TO AN ASTRONAUT WHO JUST LANDED FROM MARS?

Just park your car, man!

HOW DO YOU ORGANIZE A SPACE PARTY?

You planet!

WHICH KIND OF DINOSAURS LOVE SLEEPING?

stega-snore-us.

WHICH DAY OF THE WEEK ARE MOST TWINS BORN?

Twos-day!

WHAT DO YOU CALL AN ANGRY ICE CREAM?

A not-so-nice-cream!

WHAT DO YOU CALL A BOOMERANG THAT NEVER RETURNS BACK TO YOU?

It's a stick!

HOW DID THE MATH BOOK END UP BEING SAD?

It had sooooo many problems!

WHY DID THE MELON DECIDE TO JUMP INTO THE RIVER?

Because it wanted to be a watermelon!

NEVER TRY TO GIVE ELSA A
BALLOON.
WHY NOT?

Because she'll let it go!

IS IT ME OR DOES IT SMELL
LIKE UPDOG IN HERE?

What's updog?

NO THING MUCH, HOW ABOUT
YOU?

WHAT DID ONE PENCIL SAY TO THE OTHER PENCIL?

You're looking sharp!

HEY, HAVE YOU HEARD THE JOKE ABOUT THE SKUNK?

Don't bother . . . it stinks!

WHAT IS A FISH WITH NO EYES CALLED?

A fssssshhh!

WHY DID THE POLICE OFFICER GO TO THE BASEBALL GAME?

He heard that someone stole a base!

WHY WAS THE DOLLAR CONFUSED?

Because it didn't make cents.

WHAT KIND OF MUSICAL INSTRUMENT CAN WE FIND IN THE BATHROOM?

A tube-a toothpaste!

WHAT DO YOU CALL A COW THAT CAN PLAY MUSICAL INSTRUMENTS?

A moooo-sician!

WHAT DO YOU CALL FAKE PASTA?

An impasta!

WHY ARE GHOSTS TERRIBLE LIARS?

You can see right through them.

WHAT DO ELVES LEARN IN SCHOOL?

The elf-abet!

HOW DOES THE MOON CUT HIS HAIR?

Eclipse it!

WHAT DO YOU CALL TWO BOYS HANGING ON A CURTAIN?

Kurt and Rod!

HOW COULD YOU MAKE AN OCTOPUS LAUGH?

It's simple. With ten-tickles!

WHY DO BEES ALWAYS END UP WITH STICKY HAIR?

Because they use honey-combs!

DO YOU KNOW THE SOUND TWO HEDGEHOGS MAKE WHEN THEY HUG?

Ouch!

WHY DID THE TEDDY BEAR SAY "NO" TO DESSERT?

Because it was "stuffed!"

WHAT DID THE CALCULATOR TELL THE MATH STUDENT?

You can count on me!

WHAT DO YOU CALL AN ELDERLY SNOWMAN?

Water!

WHAT DID THE PIG SAY WHEN HE WAS IN THE SUN?

I'm bacon!

WHY WAS THE PAINTING SENT TO PRISON?

Because it was framed!

WHY COULDN'T THE SKELETON SING IN FRONT OF EVERYONE?

Because he didn't have the guts.

WHAT'S THE MIX BETWEEN A SNOWMAN AND VAMPIRE?

Frostbite!

WHY DID THE GIRL BRING A LADDER TO SCHOOL?

Because she was dying to finally go to high school!

WHAT DOES AN AVOCADO SAY WHEN IT GOES TO CHURCH?

"Holy guacamole!"

WHAT CAN YOU GET FROM A PAMPERED COW?

Spoiled milk!

WHY DID THE SALAD GO TO THE STUDIO?

To turnip the volume and listen to some beets!

WHAT KIND OF SHOES DO FROGS LOVE?

Open-toad!

WHICH DINOSAUR HAD THE GREATEST VOCABULARY?

Thesaurus!

WHAT HAPPENED WHEN THE TIGER ATE THE COMEDIAN?

He started to feel funny!

WHAT DO YOU CALL A MOUNTAIN THAT'S FUNNY?

Hill-arious!

WHAT DID THE TOILET SAY TO THE OTHER?

You look a bit flushed.

WHAT DID THE FARMER CALL HIS COW THAT FAILED TO PRODUCE MILK?

An udder failure!

WHY DID THE CHICKEN CROSS THE PLAYGROUND?

To get to the other slide!

WHAT DID 50 CENT SAY TO HIS GRANDMA AFTER SHE PRESENTED HIM WITH A SWEATER?

"Did G-Unit it?"

HOW DOES THE OCEAN SAY HELLO?

He waves!

WHAT DO YOU CALL A BULL THAT'S SLEEPING?

A bull-dozer!

WHY DID A SCHOOL BIRD GET IN TROUBLE?

For tweeting on a test!

WHY IS A FOOTBALL STADIUM ALWAYS COLD?

It has lots of fans!

WHAT KIND OF MATH DO BIRDS LOVE?

Owl-gebra!

WHERE DO MOST HORSES LIVE?

In neigh-borhoods!

HOW DOES A BARBER DRIVE TO WORK?

He takes shortcuts!

WHAT DID THE HAT SAY TO THE SCARF?

"You just hang around, and I'll go on ahead."

WHY DO DUCKS ALWAYS PAY WITH CASH?

Because they always have bills!

WHICH PLANET LOVES TO SING?

Nep-tune!

WHY DID THE PEANUT GET INTO A ROCKET?

He wanted to be an astro-nut!

WHAT DO YOU CALL A BEAR WITH NO EARS?

B!

WHAT FRUIT DO TWINS LOVE?

Pears!

WHAT KIND OF FISH WILL YOU FIND SWIMMING IN THE EVENING?

A starfish, duh!

WHY DO DRAGONS SLEEP DURING THE DAY?

So they can fight knights!

WHAT DID THE PIECE OF PAPER SAY TO THE PEN?

"Write on, dude!"

THERE IS A BOY NAMED LEE,
AND NO ONE TALKS TO HIM.
WHAT DO WE CALL HIM?

Lonely.

WHAT DID SNOW WHITE SAY
WHEN HER PHOTOS DID NOT
ARRIVE?

"Someday my prints will come!"

HOW DID THE BROOM END
UP BEING LATE?

It over swept again!

WHAT DID THE ONE ELEVATOR SAY TO THE OTHER?

I think I'm coming down with something!

WHY DOES PETER PAN FLY ALL THE TIME?

Because he Neverland-s!

WHAT'S A BANANA PEEL'S FAVORITE KIND OF SHOE?

Slippers!

WHY DID THE DINOSAUR CROSS THE ROAD?

Because chickens didn't exist yet!

WHAT IS A VAMPIRE'S FAVORITE HOLIDAY?

Fangs-giving!

WHAT DOES A MUMMY LIKE TO LISTEN TO?

"Wrap" music!

WHAT'S A SKELETON'S FAVORITE MUSICAL INSTRUMENT?

The trom-bone!

WHAT DO YOU CALL AN ELF THAT'S RICH?

Welfy!

WHY EXACTLY DID HUMPTY DUMPTY HAVE A GREAT FALL?

Because he had a horrible summer.

WHAT DID THE ONE PLATE WHISPER TO THE OTHER?

"Hey, dinner's on me."

HOW DO YOU MAKE HOLY WATER?

You boil the hell right out of it!

WHAT KIND OF TREE CAN YOU FIT IN EITHER HAND?

A palm tree, of course!

WHICH DAYS OF THE WEEK ARE THE STRONGEST?

Saturday and Sunday. The others are weekdays!

HOW CAN WE STOP A CHARGING BULL?

Just cancel its credit card!

WHY IS THE KING OF THE JUNGLE UNTRUSTWORTHY?

Because he's always lion.

WHAT DID THE TIRED TOILET
SAY TO THE FUNNY
PLUNGER?

"Gosh, I'm flushed."

WHAT DO YOU CALL A
PEPPER THAT'S NOSY?

Jalapeno business!

WHY COULDN'T COUNT
DRACULA'S WIFE SLEEP?

Because of his coffin!

WHAT DID THE EGG SAY TO THE DOCTOR?

"You just crack me up!"

WHY DID LITTLE JOHNNY EAT HIS HOMEWORK?

The teacher told him it was a piece of pie!

WHY DO HAMBURGERS TASTE BETTER OUT OF SPACE?

Because they're "meatier!"

WHY WAS THE TOMATO BLUSHING?

Because it went into its house and saw the salad dressing!

WHY DIDN'T THE DUCK PAY FOR THE LIPSTICK?

He wanted to put it on his bill!

WHY DID DARTH VADER SWITCH OFF THE LIGHT?

He prefers the dark side.

WHY DID JOHNNY THROW A
LARGE CHUNK OF BUTTER
OUT THE DOOR?

Because he wanted to see a
beautiful butter-fly!

WHAT DO YOU CALL THE
WIFE OF A HIPPIE?

A Mississippi.

WHAT STREET DO GHOSTS
HAUNT?

Dead ends.

DO YOU HAVE HOLES IN YOUR UNDERWEAR?

No . . .

So how do you put your legs through?

WHAT DID THE ONE EYE SAY TO THE OTHER?

"Between us, something smells."

WHAT'S FASTER, HOT OR COLD?

Hot. It seems like everyone catches a cold!

WHAT DO YOU CALL A FLY WITHOUT ANY WINGS?

A walk!

WHAT DID THE DALMATIAN SAY AFTER LUNCH?

That hit the spot!

WHEN DOES A JOKE TURN INTO A DAD JOKE?

When the punchline is "a parent."

HOW WOULD YOU SPEAK TO A GIANT?

By only using big words!

WHAT IS A TORNADO'S FAVORITE GAME?

Twister!

WHAT DID THE NOSE TELL THE FINGER?

"Stop picking on me!"

WHAT IS A PIRATE'S FAVORITE SUBJECT IN HIGH SCHOOL?

Arrrrrrrrrrt!

DID YOU HEAR ABOUT THE RACE BETWEEN THE BUTTER AND THE TOMATO?

I heard the tomato was trying to "catch up."

HOW CAN A TISSUE DANCE?

By putting a little boogie in it!

WHAT DO WE CALL AN ALLIGATOR THAT'S IN A VEST?

An investi-gator!

WHAT IS GREEN, HAS SIX LEGS, AND IF IT DROPS OUT OF A TREE AND FALLS ONTO YOU, IT WILL KILL YOU?

A pool table.

WHAT WOULD BEARS SAY IF THEY WERE CONFUSED?

"I bear-ly understand."

WHY DID THE COOKIE END UP IN THE HOSPITAL?

Because he felt a little crummy.

WHAT IS WORSE THAN RAINING CATS AND DOGS?

Hailing taxis!

WHAT DID THE LITTLE CORN SAY TO THE MOTHER CORN?

"Where is Pop Corn?"

WHERE DO YOU LEARN TO MAKE ICE CREAM?

Sundae school.

HOW MANY LIPS DO YOU THINK A FLOWER HAS?

It has tu-lips!

WHY CAN'T YOU TRUST ZOOKEEPERS?

They love cheetahs.

WHAT DO YOU CALL A DINOSAUR THAT CAN'T SEE?

You-think-he-saur-us?!

WHAT DO KIDS PLAY WHEN THEY CAN'T PLAY WITH A PHONE?

Bored games.

WHAT DID THE POLICEMAN SAY TO HIS TUMMY?

"Freeze! You're under a vest."

WHAT EVENT DO SPIDERS
LOVE TO ATTEND?

Webbings.

WHAT KIND OF LUNCH DO
MOMS NEVER PREPARE IN
THE MORNING?

Their own.

HEY, DID YOU HEAR THE
JOKE ABOUT THE ROOF?

Never mind, it went over your
head.

WHY DID THE GOD OF THUNDER NEED TO STRETCH HIS MUSCLES SO MUCH AS A KID?

He was a little Thor.

WHY DO BOWLING PINS HAVE SUCH A HARD LIFE?

They're always getting knocked down.

WHY ARE PENGUINS SO AWKWARD AROUND OTHERS?

Because they never seem to break the ice.

DID YOU HEAR THE STORY
ABOUT THE ACTOR WHO
SUDDENLY FELL THROUGH THE
WOODEN PLANKS ON THE
THEATER FLOOR?

I guess you could say he was just
going through a stage.

WHICH SUPERHERO ALWAYS
HITS THE MOST HOME RUNS
IN BASEBALL?

Batman!

Chapter 2: Knock-Knock Jokes

Let's have a look at some fun knock-knock jokes! A favorite among children of all ages, these jokes are knee-slappers and will keep you laughing for days!

KNOCK KNOCK!

Who's there?

JUSTIN.

Justin, who?

JUSTIN TIME FOR LUNCH, COME ON IN!

KNOCK KNOCK!

Who's there?

ORANGE.

Orange, who?

WELL, ORANGE YOU GLAD TO SEE ME TODAY?

KNOCK KNOCK!

Who's there?

SCOLD.

Scold, who?

IT FEELS SCOLD OUTSIDE, PLEASE LET ME IN!

KNOCK KNOCK!

Who's there?

LISA.

Lisa, who?

AT LISA MADE IT ON TIME!

KNOCK KNOCK!

Who's there?

EMMA.

Emma, who?

EMMA EVER GOING TO BE INVITED
INSIDE??

KNOCK KNOCK!

Who's there?

CASH.

Cash, who?

RUN FOR YOUR LIFE, IMMA CASHEW!

KNOCK KNOCK!

Who's there?

OLIVE.

Olive, who?

OLIVE HERE, GET OUT OF MY HOUSE!

KNOCK KNOCK!

Who's there?

WOODEN SHOE.

Wooden shoe, who?

WELL WOODEN SHOE LIKE TO KNOW?

KNOCK KNOCK!

Who's there?

I SMELL MOP.

I smell mop, who?

EWW, GROSS!

KNOCK KNOCK!

Who's there?

INTERRUPTING COW.

INTERRUPTING CO—

"MOOOOOOOOO!"

KNOCK KNOCK!

Who's there?

SPELL.

Spell, who?

IT'S W-H-O, NOW LET ME IN, PLEASE!

KNOCK KNOCK!

Who's there?

COW SAYS.

Cow says, who?

NO SILLY, A COW SAYS MOO!

KNOCK KNOCK!

Who's there?

ROBIN.

Robin, who?

I'M ROBIN YOU, NOW GIVE ME ALL OF
YOUR MONEY!

KNOCK KNOCK!

Who's there?

NEEDLE.

Needle, who?

I NEEDLE LITTLE HELP HERE, PLEASE
AND THANK YOU!

KNOCK KNOCK!

Who's there?

A BLUNT PENCIL.

A blunt pencil, who?

OH, NEVER MIND. IT'S A POINTLESS
END TO THE JOKE.

KNOCK KNOCK!

Who's there?

NOSE.

Nose, who?

HEY, I NOSE YOU!

KNOCK KNOCK!

Who's there?

HOWL.

Howl, who?

WELL, HOWL YOU KNOW IF YOU DON'T OPEN THE FRONT DOOR?

KNOCK KNOCK!

Who's there?

URINE.

Urine, who?

URINE BIIIIIG TROUBLE IF YOU DON'T OPEN THIS DOOR RIGHT NOW!

KNOCK KNOCK!

Who's there?

WANT.

Want, who?

WANT, WHO . . . AND THREE, FOUR,
FIVE—HIT IT!

KNOCK KNOCK!

Who's there?

A HERD.

A herd, who?

A HERD YOU WERE COMING HOME
TODAY, SO I WANTED TO VISIT!

KNOCK KNOCK!

Who's there?

CLOSURE.

Closure, who?

PLEASE CLOSURE MOUTH WHILE
YOU'RE CHEWING, IT'S RUDE!

KNOCK KNOCK!

Who's there?

CANDICE.

Candice, who?

HEY, CANDICE DOOR OPEN OR DO I
HAVE TO STAND HERE FOREVER?

KNOCK KNOCK!

Who's there?

TURNIP.

Turnip, who?

TURNIP THE VOLUME ON THE RADIO, I
LOVE THIS SONG!

KNOCK KNOCK!

Who's there?

IRAN.

Iran, who?

IRAN ALL THE WAY FROM MY HOUSE
TO SEE YOU! OPEN THE DOOR!

KNOCK KNOCK!

Who's there?

ADORE.

Adore, who?

THERE IS ADORE BETWEEN US, SO PLEASE OPEN IT!

KNOCK KNOCK!

Who's there?

MUSTACHE.

Mustache, who?

I MUSTACHE YOU AN IMPORTANT QUESTION, BUT I THINK I'D RATHER SHAVE IT FOR LATER.

KNOCK KNOCK!

Who's there?

PECAN.

Pecan, who?

WHY DON'T YOU PECAN SOMEBODY YOUR OWN SIZE?!

KNOCK KNOCK!

Who's there?

HONEYBEE.

Honeybee, who?

HONEYBEE A DEAR AND COME HELP
ME IN THE KITCHEN, PLEASE?

KNOCK KNOCK!

Who's there?

DOUBLE.

Double, who?

W.

KNOCK KNOCK!

Who's there?

MIKEY.

Mikey, who?

MIKEY DOESN'T FIT IN THE KEYHOLE,
SO OPEN THE DOOR PLEASE!

KNOCK KNOCK!

Who's there?

LITTLE OLD LADY.

Little old lady, who?

WOW, THAT WAS SOME GREAT
YODELING!

KNOCK KNOCK!

Who's there?

THEODORE.

Theodore, who?

THE ODORE WASN'T OPEN, SO I HAD
TO TRY AND KICK IT DOWN!

KNOCK KNOCK!

Who's there?

WEEKEND.

Weekend, who?

WEEKEND DO WHATEVER WE WANT!

KNOCK KNOCK!

Who's there?

RAY D.

Ray D., who?

RAY D OR NOT, HERE I COME!

KNOCK KNOCK!

Who's there?

BANANA.

Banana, who?

KNOCK KNOCK!

Who's there?

BANANA.

Banana, who?

KNOCK KNOCK!

Who's there?

BANANA.

Banana, who?

KNOCK KNOCK!

Who's there?

ORANGE.

Orange, who?

ORANGE YOU GLAD I DIDN'T SAY BANANA THIS TIME?

KNOCK KNOCK!

Who's there?

STOPWATCH.

Stopwatch, who?

JUST STOPWATCH WHAT YOU'RE
DOING AND LET ME IN ALREADY!

KNOCK KNOCK!

Who's there?

DOCTOR.

Doctor, who?

AH, I'VE SEEN THAT TV SHOW, TOO!

KNOCK KNOCK!

Who's there?

YAH.

Yah, who?

ACTUALLY, I PREFER GOOGLE.

KNOCK KNOCK!

Who's there?

NANA.

Nana, who?

IT'S NANA YOUR BUSINESS!

KNOCK KNOCK!

Who's there?

DORIS.

Doris, who?

THE DORIS LOCKED, SO OPEN UP!

Will you remember me in a year?

YES.

Will you remember me in a month?

YES.

Will you remember me in a week?

YES.

Will you remember me in a day?

YES.

KNOCK KNOCK!

Who's there?

SEE?! YOU ALREADY FORGOT ME!

Chapter 3: Riddles

Let's look at some interesting riddles that are sure to keep you highly entertained and guessing! Show these off to a friend or impress a family member with these. We'll start from easy to difficult. But don't worry—there'll be an answer page at the end. Don't cheat!

1. What five letter word becomes shorter the moment you add two letters to it?

2. Why did the girl bury her flashlight?

3. What is broken before it is used?

4. Which letter of the alphabet contains the most water?

5. What starts with the letter "P," ends in an "E," and has thousands of letters?

6. What word can begin and end with an "E" yet it only has one letter?

7. Which month has 28 days?

8. What begins with a "T," ends with a "T," and has a "T" in it?

9. What is the difference between a jeweler and a jailer?

10. What ship has two mates but no captain?

11. Timmy throws a ball as hard as he can. It comes back to him even though nothing or nobody touches it. How does this happen?

12. What is something that appears once in a full minute, twice in a precious moment, and never in a thousand years?

13. What is so fragile and delicate that saying its name breaks it?

14. They appear at night without being called and cannot be found in daytime. What are they?

15. What gets wetter the more it dries?

16. Name three consecutive days where none of the seven days of the week make an appearance.

17. What do you call a fairy that hasn't showered in a very long time?

18. Which word in the dictionary can be spelled as "incorrectly?"

19. What did the chewing gum say to the shoe?

20. What did the beach say to the tide when it came in?

21. What did the one potato chip say to the other?

22. What is something that has many rings, but no fingers?

23. What are two things that you can't have for breakfast?

24. What kind of cup cannot hold water?

25. Mrs. Green lives in her green house, Mr. Pink lives in his pink house, and Miss Red lives in the red house. But who is living in the white house?

26. Why did the little bee put honey under his pillow at night?

27. What is the longest word in the dictionary?

28. How many seconds are there in a full year?

29. If two's a company and three's a crowd, what does that make four and five?

30. What is something you will never ever see again?

31. A cloud is my mother, the wind is my father, my son is the cool stream, and my daughter is the fruit of the land. A rainbow is my bed, the earth is my final resting place, and I can make man unhappy. What am I?

32. What belongs to you but others end up using it more than you do?

33. I am taken from a mine and left in a wooden or plastic case from which I am hardly ever released, but everyone uses me. Can you guess what I am?

34. What can go up the chimney when down but cannot go down the chimney when up?

35. The Smith family is a very wealthy family. They live in a rather large, circular home. One morning, Mr. Smith woke up and saw a strawberry jam stain on his new carpet. He knew that everyone who was there that morning had a jam sandwich, so he decided to ask them all. By reading the following excuses, figure out who spilled the jam.

Billy Smith: "I was playing basketball outside!"

The maid: "Why, I was too busy dusting the corners of the house."

Chef: "I was starting to prepare lunch for everyone."

Who do you think is lying?

36. One night, a waiter, a singer, and a shoemaker go to a hotel for a few nights. When they get their bill, however, it's for four people. Who is the fourth person?

37. A dad and his son were riding their bikes and crashed. Two ambulances came and took them to different hospitals. The man's son was in the operating room and the doctor said, "I can't operate on you. You're my son." How is that possible?

38. "I have a face and hands that can move before your very eyes. Yet, when I go, my body still stands. When I stand, I lie." What am I?

39. "The skin I wear is as fine as velvet's rare. Though under the earth my house quarters are, when above it I appear. My enemies often put me in fear. At me, the gardener feels sorry. He spoils my work, and I spoil his. And that makes him worry." What am I?

40. "It was asked of me what I could be made. And so people were fed from me. It was asked of me what I could be made, and so houses were built. It was asked of me what I could be made, and so things were written. It was asked of me what I could be made, and so I fertilized the ground. But when asked more of what I could be made, there was nothing to be found." What am I?

41. Take me out and scratch my head. I am now black and warm, but I once was ruby red. What am I?

42. Where can we come across cities, towns, landmarks, shops, and streets but no people?

43. I can tire people for many hours every day. I can show you strange visions while you are away. I take your mind at night, but by day you take it back. You won't suffer to have me, but you will from my lack. What am I?

44. You use me when you're resting. I'm soft, comfortable, and I protect your neck and head. You can ask for me on an airplane, and fighting with me can be fun. What am I?

45. I can give kids a huge fright and even make them cry, but at the end they think I'm very sweet. I usually celebrate at night. What am I?

46. I am an odd number. If you take away a letter, I become even. What number am I?

47. I am light as a feather, everyone has me. However, the strongest man in the world can't seem to hold me for very long before passing out. What am I?

48. I am heavy going forward but backward I am certainly not. What am I?

49. I add lots and lots of flavor, and I have so many layers, but if you get too close to me, I can make you cry. What am I?

50. I often follow you and I copy your every move. Yet, you can never catch me or even touch me. What am I?

51. What can be broken, even if it is never picked up or touched?

52. I am a little seed with three letters in my name. If you remove the last two letters, I will still sound the same. What am I?

53. What can go up but can never come back down?

54. You go at red, but stop at green. What am I?

55. I have many teeth but I can't bite. I'm often used early but rarely at night. What am I?

56. I can never be thrown, but I can be caught. Ways to lose me are always being sought. What am I?

57. I'm (usually) white and used for cutting and grinding. When I'm damaged, humans usually remove me or fill me. I've proven to be quite useful for most animals. What am I?

58. I'm forever hungry, and I will die if I'm not usually fed; whatever I touch always turns red. What am I?

59. I sound like one letter but I'm written with three. I show you things when you look through me. What am I?

60. I can be made, saved, changed, and raised. What am I?

61. I'm so fast, travelling nearly 100 miles per hour, but I never leave the room. When you cover me, it doesn't slow me down. You have no way of knowing if I come only once or again and again. What am I?

62. I had people walk all over me before, but not many did. I can never stay full for long. Like many things, I can be light and dark. What am I?

63. I look exactly like you, but I can never be you. You can blow me up or find me in a house. Whether you share me or frame me, it would be a nice gift for someone. What am I?

64. I can be red or blue or any other color—I am in constant change. I can make you feel happy or completely terrible. I'm always by your side except when you're sleeping. What am I?

Answer Page

1. Short.
2. Because the batteries died.
3. Egg.
4. C.
5. The post office.
6. Envelope
7. All of them, duh!
8. A teapot!
9. A jeweler sells watches, a jailer watches cells.
10. A relationship!
11. He throws it straight up!
12. The letter M.
13. Silence.
14. Stars.
15. Towel.
16. Yesterday, today and tomorrow.
17. Stinker bell.
18. Incorrectly.
19. I'm stuck on you.
20. Long time, no sea.
21. Let's go for a dip.
22. Telephone.

23. Lunch and dinner.
24. A cupcake!
25. The president.
26. He wanted to have sweet
    dreams.
27. Smiles!! There is a mile
    between each "s."
28. January 2nd, February 2nd,
    March 2nd, April 2nd .
29. Nine.
30. Yesterday.
31. Rain.
32. Pencil.
33. Pencil lead!
34. An umbrella.
35. It was the maid! Because they
    live in a circular house, there
    are no corners.
36. One night actually means one
    "knight." That makes it four.
37. The doctor is his mom.
38. Clock.
39. Mole.
40. Tree.

41. Match.
42. A map.
43. Sleep.
44. A pillow.
45. Halloween.
46. Seven.
47. Your breath.
48. A ton.
49. Onion.
50. A shadow.
51. A promise.
52. Pea.
53. Your age.
54. A watermelon.
55. A comb.
56. A cold.
57. Tooth.
58. Fire.
59. Eye.
60. Money.
61. A sneeze.
62. The moon.
63. A photo of you.
64. Your mood.

Chapter 4: Long Jokes

1. I just bought myself a new blindfold. I can't see myself wearing it.

2. If you think swimming with dolphins is expensive? You should try swimming with sharks. Cost me an arm and a leg!

3. Customer: "Waiter! Waiter! There's a fly drowning in my soup." Waiter: "Well, don't look at me. I didn't teach it how to swim."

4. While leaving a grocery store, a customer dropped a bag of flour. A Boy Scout ran to pick it up. "Don't bother, young man," said the customer. "It's self-rising."

5. Johnny: "Why does the new baby at your house cry so much, Tommy?"
Tommy: "It doesn't cry that much—and, anyway, if all your teeth were out, your hair off, and your legs so weak you couldn't stand on them, guess you'd feel like crying yourself!"

6. "Can your little baby brother talk yet?"
    A kind neighbor asked a young boy.
    "No, he can't talk, and there's no reason
    why he should talk!" was the young boy's
    reply.
    "Why would he want to talk when all he
    has to do is scream and yell to get
    everything he wants in this house?"

7. Aunt Eliza came up the walk and said to
    her small nephew, "Good morning, Willie.
    Is your mother in?"
    "Sure she's in," replied Willie. "Do you
    think I'd be working in the garden on
    Saturday morning if she wasn't?"

8. Mrs. Jones was getting dinner ready when in
    came little Fred with a happy smile on his
    face.
    "What has Mamma's darling been doing this
    morning?" asked his mother.
    "I have been playing Postman," replied little
    Fred.
    "Postman?" exclaimed his mother. "How
    could you do that when you had no letters?"
    "Oh, but I had," replied Fred. "I was looking

in your trunk up in your room and I found
a packet of letters tied with a ribbon,
and I posted one under every door in the
street."

9. A little boy finds a magical lamp. He rubs
the lamp, and a genie appears and says,
"What is your first wish?"
The boy says, "I wish I were rich!"
The genie replies, "And it is done! What
is your second wish, Rich?"

10. Timmy asks Jenny to go to the dance.
She agrees, and he decides to rent a
suit. The rental has a long line, so he
waits and waits, and finally he gets his
suit. He decides to buy some flowers for
her, so he goes to the flower shop. The
flower shop has a long line, so he
patiently waits and waits, until he finally
is able to buy some. He picks up Jenny
and they proceed to go to the dance.
There is a very long line into the dance,
so they wait and wait. Finally, they get
into the dance, and the guy offers to get

the girl a drink. She asks for some punch, so he goes to the drink table, and there is no punch line.

11. A guy is sitting at home when he hears a knock at the door. He opens the door and sees a snail on the porch. He picks up the snail and throws it as far as he can. A year later, there's another knock at the door. He opens it and sees the same snail. The snail says, "What was that all about?"

12. A young man was driving down the street when a police officer suddenly stopped him in his tracks. The officer looked in the back of the man's truck, appearing confused, and asked, "Sir, why do you have penguins in your truck?"
The man said, "Well, Officer, these are MY penguins. They belong to me."
"You need to take them to the zoo at once," the police officer said.
A few days later, the officer saw the same guy driving down the road.

He pulled him over again. He saw that the penguins were still in the truck but wearing sunglasses this time around. "I thought I told you to take those penguins to the zoo!" the officer said. "Oh I did," the man replied. "Today, I decided to take them to the beach."

13. Three friends find themselves stuck in the desert due to their car breaking down suddenly. They decided to hike to town, and each takes something with them. One guy takes a big jug of water. The second guy decides to take a few sandwiches. The last guy takes one of the car doors.
The first guy says to the last one, "I'm bringing the water because if I get thirsty, I can take a sip. Plus, it definitely would be wise to bring a sandwich in case we get hungry, but why are you bringing a car door?"
The last guy replies, "Well, if I get hot, I can just roll down the window."

14. An old man arrives at his favorite
restaurant, goes to the table he usually
likes to sit in, and orders the usual—a
delicious bowl of miso soup. The waiter
brings the soup and sets it down in front
of him, standing back to watch the old
man enjoy it. But the old man just sits
there and does nothing.
"Is there something wrong, sir?" the
waiter asks after a few minutes.
"I can't eat this soup!" the man replies.
"Is the soup too hot?" the waiter asks.
"No."
"Too cold?"
"Nope."
"Too salty?"
"Not at all."
"Too sweet?"
"No."
The waiter calls the head waiter, and the
chef, and explains the situation to them.
They both go through the same routine
with the old man:
"Too hot?" "Too cold?"
"No, no, no."

Finally the chef, confused and at his wits end, says, "Sir, I will taste the soup myself. Where is the spoon?"
The old man says, "A-ha!"

15. A chicken marches into the local library, walks up to the front desk, and says, "Book, book, book!"
The librarian hands over a couple of children's paperbacks and watches the chicken as it leaves the library, walks across the street, through the soccer field, and disappears down the hill.
The next day, the chicken is back. It walks right up to the librarian, drops the books on her desk, and says, "Book, Book, BOOK!" The librarian hands over a few books and again watches the chicken drag them away. The next day, the chicken comes for a third time.
It drops the books on the desk and says, "Book, Book, Book, BOOK!" This time, once the chicken leaves the building, the librarian, who is confused at this point, decides to follow it—across the street,

through the soccer field, and down the hill to a small pond. On a rock on the edge of the pond is the biggest frog the librarian has ever seen.

The chicken walks up to the frog, drops the book on the pond's edge, and says, "Book, Book, Book!"

The frog hops over and says, "Read it, read it, read it . . ."

16. A boy asks his father, "Dad, is it good to eat insects?"

"That's disgusting—don't talk about things like that over dinner," the dad replies.

After dinner, the father asks, "Now, son, what is it that you wanted to ask me?"

"Oh, nothing," the boy says.

"There was a fly in your soup, but now it's gone."

17. Sherlock Holmes and Dr. Watson decided to camp for a few nights. They pitched their tent under the stars and went straight to bed.

Sometime in the middle of the night, Holmes wakes Watson up and says, "Watson, look up at the stars, and tell me what you see."

Watson replied, "I see millions upon millions of stars."

Holmes said, "And what can be deduced from that?"

Watson replied, "Well, if there are millions of stars, and even some that have planets, it's quite likely there are a few planets like Earth out there. And if there are a few planets like Earth out there, there might also be life. It wouldn't make sense that we are the only anomaly."

Holmes screams, "Watson, YOU IDIOT! IT MEANS THAT SOMEONE STOLE OUR TENT!"

18. There was a young boy who visited the local barber shop every Saturday afternoon.

On one of the boy's regular visits, the barber notices him and whispers to

another customer, "This is the dumbest boy in the world! Watch, I'll prove it!" The barber puts a one-dollar bill in his one hand and two quarters in the other. He then calls the boy over and asks, "Which one do you want, son?"
The boy takes the quarters in his other hand and leaves. "Well, what did I tell you?" said the barber.
"That boy will never learn!" Later, when the customer leaves the barbershop, he sees the same young boy coming out of the nearby ice cream shop.
"Hey, son! May I ask you a question?"
"Sure!" the boy said.
"Why did you take the two quarters instead of the dollar bill?"
The boy licked his cone before replying, and said, "Because the day I take the dollar, then the game is over!"

19. A 55-year-old man was born on May 5, has been married 5 years, has 5 children, makes $55, 555.55 a year, and trusts the number 5. One day a friend tells the

man that a horse named Lucky 5 will be running in the fifth race at the local track that evening. Excitedly, the man withdraws $5,555.00 cash from his bank account, goes to the races and bets on Lucky 5. Sure enough, the horse comes in fifth.

20. A police officer was testing three dumb brothers who were all aspiring detectives and were put in training to become one. To test their skills in being able to recognize a suspect, the police officer shows the first brother a picture for a short period of time and then hides it. "Now, let's say this is your suspect. How would you recognize him?" asks the police officer.
The first brother answers, "Oh, that's easy officer, we'll be able to catch him quickly because he only has one eye!"
The police officer says, "Well, umm, that's because the picture I showed you is his side profile. The picture is being taken from the side, so he only has one

eye."
Shocked by this ridiculous answer, he shows the picture for a few seconds to the second brother and again, asks, "This is your suspect, how would you recognize him?"
The second brother smiles and says, Ha! He'd be far too easy to catch because he only has one ear!"
The police officer angrily responds, "Is this a joke? What's the matter with the two of you? Of course only one eye and one ear are showing because it's a picture of his side profile! Is that really the best answer you can come up with?"
Extremely frustrated by the time he starts finishing up, he shows the picture to the third brother and again asks, "This is your suspect, now how would you recognize him?"
He quickly adds, "Think hard before giving me a dumb answer!"
The brother looks at the picture quietly for a moment and says, "Hmm . . . the suspect wears contact lenses."

The police officer, appearing surprised and speechless, asks the third brother if he is certain of his answer because he really doesn't know if the suspect wears contacts or not.
"Well that's a very interesting answer. Wait here for a few minutes, I'm just going to check his file, and I'll get back to you on that." He leaves the room and goes to his office, checks the suspect's file in his computer and comes back with a beaming smile on his face.
"Wow! I can't believe it. It's TRUE! The suspect does in fact wear contact lenses. Good work! How did you know this?"
"That's easy", the brother said.
"He can't wear glasses because he only has one eye and one ear!"

21. One day, there was an elderly couple who noticed that they were getting a lot more forgetful about everything, so they decided to go to the doctor. The doctor advised them to start writing things down so they don't forget. They went

home and the old lady kindly asked her
husband to get her some vanilla ice
cream.
"You might want to write it down honey,
so that you don't forget," she said.
The husband said, "No, don't worry, I'll
be able to remember."
She then told her husband she wanted a
bowl of ice cream with some whipped
cream. "Please write it down," she asked
him.
Again, he said, "No, no, I can remember.
You'd like a bowl of ice cream with
whipped cream."
Then the old lady said she wants a bowl
of ice cream with whipped cream, a
cherry on top, and some chocolate sauce.
"I think it would be better to write it
down, just in case." she told her husband.
And again he said, "No, it's okay, I got it.
You want a bowl of ice cream with
whipped cream, a cherry on top, and
some chocolate sauce."
So he finally goes to get her ice cream
and spends a very long time in the

kitchen, over 45 minutes. He comes out of the kitchen to his wife and hands her a plate of bacon, tomato, and eggs.
The old wife stares at the plate for a moment, then looks at her husband and asks, "Where's the toast and jam?"

22. So I was sitting on the bus just reading a book when somebody gently tapped me on the shoulder to get my attention. I turned around and saw an old lady.
She said to me, "Son, would you like some nuts? I've got a couple of cashews and almonds if you'd like."
"Sure I'd like some, thank you," I replied. She gave me a handful of nuts and went back to sit with her friends.
What a nice lady! I thought while happily munching on the nuts.
I felt another tap on my shoulder a few minutes later, and to no surprise, it was the kind old lady again. She offered me some nuts. I gladly accepted and she went back to her seat.
After about 15 minutes, she tapped me

on the shoulder, once again offering some nuts.

I asked her, "Why don't you eat them yourself?"

"Because we've got no teeth, sonny." she replied.

"Oh, I see . . . then why do you buy them?" I asked.

"Oh, we just love to suck the chocolate off of them."

23. Mom: Time to wake up and go to school!
Son: No, I don't wanna go to school today!
Mom: You have to go to school!
Son: But I don't wanna go to school, mom!
Mom: Give me three good reasons why you should stay at home, and I will give you three good reasons why you need to go to school.
Son: Well, all the students hate me, the teachers hate me, and . . . and . . . I just don't wanna go!
Mom: Well, for one, I have a lot to do

today, and I can't take care of you
today, as well. Two, you are over 40
years old, and three, you are the
principal!

24. An old, tired-looking dog wanders into a
guy's front yard. The guy looks at the
dog's collar and sees he has a home. He
decides to feed the poor thing. The dog
follows him into the house, goes down
the hall, jumps on the couch, gets
comfortable, and soon falls asleep. The
man thinks this is rather odd but lets
him sleep anyways. After about an hour
the dog wakes up, walks to the door, and
the guy lets him out. The dog wags his
tail and leaves. The next day the dog
comes back and scratches at the door.
The guy opens the door, the dog comes
in, goes down the hall, jumps on the
couch, gets comfortable, and falls asleep.
The man lets him sleep again. After
about an hour, the dog wakes up and the
same thing happens—he walks to the
door and the guy lets him out. The dog

wags his tail and leaves. This goes on for days. The guy becomes curious, so he pins a note on the dog's collar that says, "Your dog has been taking a nap at my house every day."

The next day, the dog arrives with another note stuck to his collar: "He lives in a home with five children and the poor thing is just trying to catch up on his sleep. Do you mind if I come with him tomorrow?"

25. I was having trouble with my computer. So, I called Joseph, a nice 14-year-old boy who lives next door, to come over. Joseph solved the problem by clicking a few buttons here and there. As he was going back home, I called after him and asked, "So, what was the problem?"

He said, "Oh, it was just an ID ten T error"

I did not want to seem stupid, so I asked, "An ID ten T error? What's that? Just in case I need to fix it again."

Joseph smiled, and said, "Haven't you

heard of an ID ten T error before?"

"No," I replied.

"Write it down," he said, "and I think you'll figure it out."

So I wrote it down: I D 10 T. I used to really like that little boy.

26. Two friends are out fishing for the day, but unfortunately, they've had no luck catching anything yet. Then, another fisherman walks by with a giant net of fish.

They ask him, "Excuse me, but, where did you get all those fish?"

The fisherman replies, "Well, if you just go down the stream until the water isn't salty, you'll find plenty of fish! It's like a gold mine!"

"Thank you, sir!" the one friend says, and they part ways.

15 minutes later, one friend says to the other, "Fill the bucket up with water" and see if the water is salty."

He dips the bucket in the stream and drinks some. "Nope. Still salty."

30 minutes later, he asks him to check again.

"Nope, it's still salty."

One hour later they check again. "Nope, still salty."

"Well that's just great," the first friend finally says. "We have been trying to catch fish for almost two hours and the water is still salty!"

"I know," says the other. "And the bucket is almost empty!"

27. A prince was put under a spell so that he could speak only one word each year. However, if the prince did not speak for two years, the following year he could speak two words, and so on. One day, he fell in love with a beautiful lady. He did not speak for two whole years so that in the next year, he could call her "my darling." But then, he wanted to tell her he loved her, so he waited three more years. At the end of these five years, he wanted to ask her to marry him, so he waited another four years. Finally, as the

ninth year of silence ended. He took the lady to the most romantic place in the whole kingdom and said, "My darling, I love you! Will you marry me?"
To that, the lady said, "Hmm? Pardon?"

28. A teacher is trying to teach her class the definition of the word "definitely."
"Does anyone want to try and give me an example?" she asks.
Young Suzie raises her hand and says, "The grass is definitely green!"
"Well, sometimes the grass can be brown or yellow," The teacher says.
"Anyone else want to give it a shot?"
"Hmm . . . the sky is definitely blue," says little Timmy.
"Well, Timmy, the sky can be gray when it's cloudy or black when it's dark at night," says the teacher.
In the front of the class, Johnny raises his hand and asks, "Do farts have lumps?"
Shocked, the teacher says, "Why, no, absolutely not!"

Johnny then says, "Well then, I definitely pooped my pants!"

29. Three friends find themselves stranded on a deserted island. After a while, they discover a magic lamp and decide to rub it. A genie appears and the genie agrees to grant each friend one wish.
"I want to go home; I miss my family!" says the first friend. The genie grants her wish.
"I want to go home, too!" says the second friend. And the genie sends her back home too.
"I'm lonely," says the third friend. "I really wish my friends were back here with me."

30. A man walks into a library, approaches the librarian, and says, "I'll have a cheeseburger and fries, please."
The librarian says, "Sir, you know you're in a library, right?"
"Sorry," he whispers. "I'll have a cheeseburger and fries, please."

31. A frantic man takes his sick little
    Chihuahua to the vet. When they arrive,
    they're immediately taken to a room in
    the back. Soon after that, a cute
    Labrador dog walks in, sniffs the
    Chihuahua for around 10 minutes and
    leaves. Then, an adorable Tabby cat
    comes in, stares at the Chihuahua for 10
    more minutes, and leaves. Finally, the
    doctor comes in, gives some medicine and
    hands the man a $250 bill.
    "This must be a mistake," the man says.
    "I've only been here for 20 minutes!"
    "Oh there's no mistake," the doctor says.
    "It's $100 for the lab test, $100 for the
    cat scan, and $50 for the medicine."

32. A cruise ship passes by a remote island,
    and all the passengers see a bearded man
    running around, waving his arms about
    and screaming.
    "Captain," one passenger asks. "Who is
    that man over there?"
    "I honestly have no idea," the captain
    says. "But he goes absolutely nuts every
    year when we pass him!"

33. Two best friends are walking their dogs—a huge Dalmatian and a small Chihuahua—when they suddenly smell something delicious coming from a restaurant nearby.

The girl with the Dalmatian says, "Hey, let's get something to eat. I'm starving!"

But the girl with the Chihuahua says, "We can't go in there, we have our dogs with us."

So the first girl says, "Just follow my lead. I have an idea." She puts on a pair of sunglasses and walks into the restaurant.

"Sorry ma'am," says the owner, "no pets allowed."

"But this is my guide dog," the girl with the Dalmatian says.

"A Dalmatian?"

"Yes, they're using them now."

The owner says, "Very well then, come on in."

The girl with the Chihuahua repeats the process and gets the same response from the owner: "Sorry, no pets allowed."

"But this is my guide dog," says the
second girl.
"A Chihuahua?" asks the confused owner.
"A Chihuahua?!" says the girl in the dark
glasses. "They actually gave me a
Chihuahua?!"

34. A snail goes to buy a car. The salesman is
    surprised when the snail picks out a fast,
    expensive sports car. He's even more
    surprised when the snail wanted a big
    red "S" to be painted on both sides of
    the car.
    "Why would you want such a thing?"
    asked the salesman.
    The snail replied, "I really want people to
    say, 'Look at that S car go!'"

35. A guy who's looking for work decides to
    knock on every door asking for a job.
    After a while, he goes to a house, asks
    for a job and the homeowner hands him a
    brush and a can of paint and offers him
    $150 to paint his porch. A few hours
    later, the guy comes back to the

homeowner and says, "I've finished, but I hope you know that your car's a Ferrari, not a Porsche."

36. John visited his 90-year-old grandpa who lived way out in the country. On the first morning of the visit, John's grandpa prepared a breakfast of bacon and eggs. John noticed some dirt on his plate, and asked, "Are these plates clean?"
His grandpa replied, "These plates are as clean as cold water can get them. Just go ahead and finish your meal." For lunch, Grandpa made some grilled chicken and salad.
Again, John felt concerned about the cleanliness of the plates, as his plate appeared to have specks of dried egg on it. "Are you sure these plates are clean?" he asked.
Without looking up, Grandpa said, "I told you before, those dishes are as clean as cold water can get them!" Later, as John was leaving, his grandpa's dog started to bark at him and wouldn't let him pass.

John said, "Grandpa, your dog won't let me get by!"

Grandpa yelled to the dog, "Cold Water, go lie down!"

37. Einstein sits next to a man on a very long flight.

    Einstein says, "Hey, how about we play a game? I'll ask you a question, and if you don't know the answer to it, you will pay me only $5. You'll do the same; you'll ask me a question, but if I don't know the answer, I will pay you $500." The man agrees and the game starts.

    Einstein asks the first question, "What is the distance between the Earth and the Sun?" The man doesn't say a word. He reaches into his pocket, and pulls out $5. He then asks Einstein, "What goes up a hill with two legs but comes down on three?" Einstein thinks about it for a long time, but fails to answer the question. After almost an hour, he gives the man $500.

    Einstein, feeling angry and irritated then

asks, "Well, so what goes up a hill on two legs and comes down on three?"
The man reaches into his pocket and gives Einstein $5.

38. A woman had twin babies and fell asleep immediately after. A couple of weeks later, she finally wakes up and asks the doctor, "Where are my babies?"
The doctor replies, "They are both fine, you have a beautiful boy and girl. Your husband went back to work and you were out so long that your brother named them." Because her brother was not very clever, the woman was concerned.
"Oh no. What did he name them?"
"He named the girl Denise," the doctor replied.
The woman felt relieved, "Well, that's not so bad. What about the boy?"
"Denephew."

39. An elderly couple had been married for more than 65 years. They shared everything. They talked about

everything. They kept secrets from each other, except that the old woman had a big box in the top of her closet. She told her husband to never open it or ask her about it. For all these years, he never thought about opening the box, but one day the old woman got very sick. Trying to sort out their documents, the old man took the box and brought it to his wife's bedside. It was time that her husband knew what exactly was in the box. She told him to open it, and when he did, he found two cute dolls (that the old woman made herself) and a stack of money that amounted to $95,000. He asked her about the contents of the box.

"When we were going to be married," she said, "my grandmother told me the secret of a happy marriage. She told me that we must not argue. If I ever got angry with you, I should just keep quiet and make a doll instead"

The old man was so happy, he almost cried. Only two precious dolls were in that box. She had only been angry with

him twice in all those years of their
happy, loving marriage.
"Honey," he said, "that explains the doll,
but what about the money? Where did it
come from?"
"Oh," she said, "That's the money I
made from selling the rest of the dolls"

40. One day, three turtles by the name of
Joe, Steve, and Poncho, decide to go on a
picnic. Joe packs the picnic basket with
their favorite food and drinks—cookies,
potato chips, bottled soda, and
sandwiches. The problem is, the picnic
site is 10 miles away, so the turtles would
take 10 days to get there. They embark
on the journey, and by the time they
finally arrive at the picnic site,
everyone's tired and hungry. Steve takes
everything out of the basket, one by one.
When he takes out the sodas, he realizes
that Joe forgot to bring the bottle
opener for the sodas! Joe and Steve
plead with Poncho to go back home and
get it, but Poncho says no, knowing that

they'll have eaten all the food by the time he gets back.Somehow, after two long hours of talking, the turtles manage to convince Poncho to go, swearing on their great-great-great-grand turtles' graves that they won't have a single bite to eat. So, Poncho sets off down the road, slow and steady. 20 days and nights pass but no Poncho. At this point, Joe and Steve are starving, but a promise is a promise. Another day passes and still no Poncho, but they remember that a promise is a promise. After three more days pass without Poncho in sight, Steve starts getting impatient.

"I NEED FOOD!" he says.

"NO!" said Joe. "We promised, remember?"

Five more days pass. Joe realizes that Poncho probably went to a restaurant down the road, so the two turtles open the basket, get a sandwich, and open their mouths to eat. Right at that moment, Poncho suddenly appears behind a rock.

"Well, just for that, I'm not going!"

41.   Betty was a little old lady who was
always cheerful and quite happy with her
life. Lately, though, she started having a
bit of a problem. One day, she went to
the doctor and said, "I have a problem
with gas, but it really doesn't bother me
all that much. My farts never smell and
are always silent."
The doctor replied, "Is that so?"
Betty continued, "Yes! As a matter of
fact, I've farted at least 20 times since
I've been here in your tiny office. You
didn't know I was farting because they
don't smell, and they stay silent."
The doctor said, "I see. Take these pills
and make sure to come back to see me
next week."
Betty went home and took her pills from
the doctor, and suddenly she started
seeing some big changes in her everyday
life. The next week, she went back to
the doctor.
"Doctor," she says, "I don't know what
on earth you gave me, but now my farts,
although still silent, stink terribly."

The doctor nods and says, "Good! Now that we've cleared up your sinuses, let's work on your hearing."

42. "What does your dad do for a living again? "asked the school secretary, filling in the forms at the start of the school year.
"He's a magician," said the small boy.
"How interesting! What's his favorite trick?"
"He likes cutting people in half with a saw!"
"Really? Now, next question. Do you have any brothers or sisters?"
"Yes, one half brother and two half-sisters."

43. A lion woke up one morning feeling really bored, so he decided to be mean to all the animals. He went out, cornered a small innocent armadillo, and roared, "Who is the mightiest of all jungle animals?!"

The scared and trembling armadillo says, "You are, mighty lion!"

Later, the lion confronts a fox and asks, "Who is the mightiest of all jungle animals?"

On a roll now, the lion appears in front of a gigantic elephant and roars, "Who is mightiest of all jungle animals?"

Fast as lightning, an elephant then snatches up the lion with his trunk, slams him hard against a tree many times, leaving the lion feeling hurt and weak. The elephant then stomps on the lion until he manages to finally get away.

The lion, roaring in pain, lifts his head and tells the elephant, "Hey, just because you're clueless and don't know the answer, you don't have to get so upset about it!"

Chapter 5: Tongue Twisters

Try these fun tongue twisters! We'll start with easy ones just to get you warmed up. Try saying them as fast as you can and challenge your friends!

1. A proper copper coffee pot.

2. Zebras zig and zebras zag.

3. He threw three balls.

4. Greek grapes, Greek grapes, Greek grapes.

5. Lucky rabbits like to cause a ruckus.

6. Cooks cook cupcakes quickly.

7. Six sticky skeletons.

8. Nine nimble noblemen nibbling nuts.

9. Bouncing bed bugs.

10. Crisp crusts crackle and crunch.

11. Really leery, rarely Larry.

12. Twelve twins twirled twelve twigs.

13. Scissors sizzle, thistles sizzle.

14. Which witch is which?

15. Daddy draws doors.

16. Knox in box. Fox in socks.

17. Billy Bob boldly blabbered about
the baby boy.

18. Red lorry, yellow lorry, red lorry,
yellow lorry.

19. Mixing a box of mixed biscuits with
a boxed biscuit mixer.

20. Rory's rake rarely rakes right
really.

21. She sold seven shabby sheared
sheep on ships.

22. If you are noticing this notice, you
will notice that noticing this notice
is not worth noticing.

23. You'll find the buttered bucket bottom at the bottom of the butter bucket.

24. Sport shops stock short spotted socks.

25. Merry music made by many mumbling mice in the moonlight.

26. Do not light a night-light on a night as light as tonight.

27. Shave a single shingle thin.

28. Susie was seen singing in a shoeshine shop.

Now, let's move onto harder tongue twisters. Try to keep up!

29. Tommy tossed his tenth tooth when it turned twelve times.

30. Shells of selfish shellfish surprised shrieking Shirley.

31. Kitty caught the kitten in the kitchen.

32. We surely shall see the sunshine soon.

33. Six slimy snails slid slowly seaward.

34. Four furious friends fought for the phone.

35. Which wristwatches are Swiss wristwatches?

36. Four frantic fragile frogs fled from fifty fierce fish.

37. Six thin things seven thick things too.

38. Rugged Ricky ran from raging rams.

39. And when they battle in a puddle, it's a tweetle beetle puddle battle.

40. How much wood could a woodchuck chuck if a woodchuck could chuck wood?

41. A tweetle beetle noodle poodle doodle bottled paddled muddled duddled fuddled wuddled muzzled fox in socks, sir!

42. If Peter Piper picked a peck of pickled peppers, where's the peck of pickled peppers Peter Piper picked?

43. Luke Luck likes lakes. Luke's duck likes lakes. Luke Luck licks lollipops. Luck's duck licks lollipops.

44. Betty bought butter but the butter was bitter so Betty bought better butter to make the bitter butter better, and the bitter butter became better butter!

45. She surely sells seashells by the seashore.

46. Fuzzy Wuzzy was a bear, with no hair so to be fair, Fuzzy Wuzzy wasn't a very fuzzy bear.

47. Black bug bleeds black blood, blue
bug bleeds blue blood.

48. Two witches were watching two
watches, so which witch would
watch which watch?

49. A skunk that stunk sat on a stump
and thunk the stump stunk, but the
stump thunk the skunk was a punk
who stunk.

50. I thought a thought, but the
thought that I thought was not the
thought that I thought I thought.
If the thought I thought I thought
had been the thought that I
thought, I wouldn't have thought at
all.

51. Lesser leather never weathered
wetter weather better.

52. If you must cross a coarse cross
cow across a crowded cow crossing,
cross the cross coarse cow across
the crowded cow crossing carefully.

53. Dick Pickens pricked his pinkie
pickling cheap cling peaches in an
inch of Pinch and framed his famed
French finch photos.

54. What would Chester cheetah chew
and chunk on? Well, Chester
cheetah chewed a chunk of cheap
cheddar cheese and the chunk of
cheese chunked Chester cheetah.

55. While a doctor doctors another
doctor, does the doctor doing the
doctoring, doctor as the doctor
being doctored wants to be
doctored or does the doctor doing
the doctoring doctor as he wants to
doctor?

56. Seven swans swam over the sea,
swim, swans, swim! Seven swans
swam back again, well swum, swans.

Conclusion

Are you ready to make everyone around you laugh hysterically? Whether that's impressing your friends, making your family members laugh, getting your boring old teacher to crack a smile, or perhaps an elderly neighbor down the road could use some cheering up, I hope you'll find the jokes in this book fun and joyful to read. Be sure to share these great jokes with others and don't forget to give this book a rating! See you next time!

REFERENCES

Baardsen, D., Lubarsky, R., & Campanaro, D. (2019, September 7). 235+ Hilarious Jokes For Kids That Adults Find Funny Too. Scary Mommy. https://www.scarymommy.com/best-jokes-for-kids/

Bounce Patrol - Kids Songs. (2015). 20 Kids Jokes! Funny Jokes for Children | Bounce Patrol [YouTube Video]. On YouTube. https://www.youtube.com/watch?v=cK1LdvpglsE

Clean Jokes – Page 2 – Jokes Of The Day. (n.d.). Jokesoftheday.com. Retrieved March 18, 2021, from https://jokesoftheday.com/funnyjokes/clean/page/2/

Fanning, C. E., & Wilson, H. W. (1916). Toaster's handbook : jokes, stories, and quotations. H.W. Wilson.

Long Jokes -- Laugh at 4,300 Funny Kids Jokes by Boys' Life. (n.d.). Jokes by Scout Life. https://jokes.scoutlife.org/jokes/long-jokes/

LONG RIDDLES for kids (with answers). (2019). Www.pocoyo.com. https://www.pocoyo.com/en/riddles/long

Marion Dix Mosher. (1932). More toasts. H.W. Wilson.

Nelson, A. (2019, July 24). 110 of the best jokes for kids that are actually funny. Inews.co.uk. https://inews.co.uk/light-relief/jokes/jokes-kids-funny-159437

Smith, B. (2013, July 15). 19 Clean Jokes To Tell Your Kids...That Are Actually Funny. BuzzFeed. https://www.buzzfeed.com/bensmith/clean-jokes-to-tell-your-kids-that-are-actually-funny

The Book of riddles. (1846). J.F. Brown.